MAMMALS

Text by Sarah Lovett

John Muir Publications
Santa Fe, New Mexico

Special thanks to
Kent Newton, Curator of Mammals, Albuquerque Zoo
Bonnie Jacobs, Primate Consultant
Bat Conservation International

John Muir Publications, P.O. Box 613, Santa Fe, New Mexico 87504

First edition. Second printing September 1994

Printed on recycled paper

Library of Congress Cataloging-in-Publication Data

Lovett, Sarah, 1953–
    Mammals / text by Sarah Lovett. — 1st ed.
      p. cm. — (Extremely weird)
    Includes index.
    Summary: Describes several unusual mammals,
including the Tasmanian devil, three-toed sloth,
anteater, and musk-ox.
    ISBN 1-56261-107-0 : $9.95
    1. Mammals—Miscellanea—Juvenile literature.
[1. Mammals.] I. Title. II. Series: Lovett, Sarah, 1953–
Extremely weird.
QL706.2.L66 1993
599—dc20   93-14844
                          CIP

Illustrations: Mary Sundstrom, Beth Evans   AC
Design: Sally Blakemore
Typography: Ken Wilson, John Muir Publications
Printer: Guynes Printing of New Mexico
Bindery: Prizma Industries, Inc.

Distributed to the book trade by
W. W. Norton & Co., Inc.
500 Fifth Avenue
New York, New York 10110

Distributed to the education market by
Wright Group Publishing, Inc.
19201 120th Avenue N.E.
Bothell, Washington 98011-9512

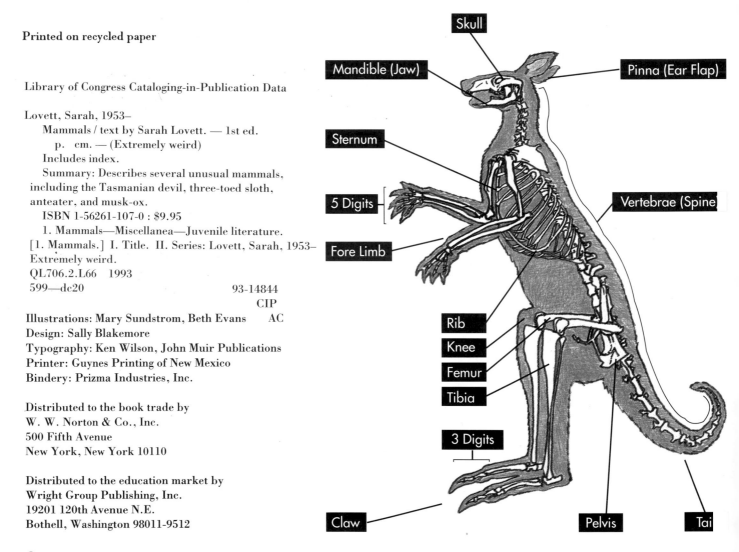

Cover:
Slender-tailed Meerkat *Suricata suricatta*

Sunbathing and perching like prairie dogs are favorite activities of slender-tailed meerkats. These very social mammals live in colonies of ten to 15 individuals. Meerkats live in Africa, and they eat insects, small vertebrates, eggs, and some greenery. Meerkats use more than ten vocal sounds, including a threat growl and an alarm bark, to communicate.

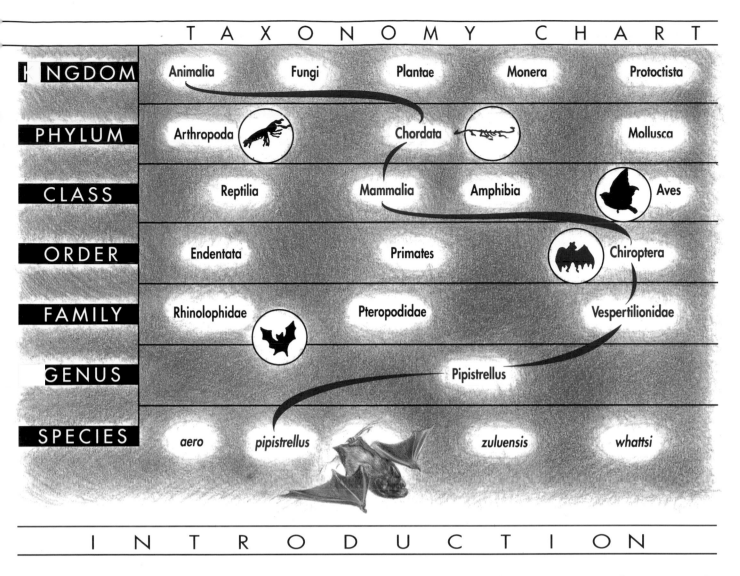

KINGDOM	Animalia	Fungi	Plantae	Monera	Protoctista
PHYLUM	Arthropoda	Chordata		Mollusca
CLASS	Reptilia	Mammalia	Amphibia	Aves
ORDER	Endentata	Primates	Chiroptera
FAMILY	Rhinolophidae	Pteropodidae	Vespertilionidae
GENUS		Pipistrellus
SPECIES	*aero*	*pipistrellus*	*zuluensis*	*whattsi*

I N T R O D U C T I O N

What do the thimble-sized bumblebee bat and the 170-ton blue whale have in common? If you guessed they both belong to the scientific order *Mammalia*, you're right. They're both mammals.

Mammals—including us humans—are the only animals that breathe air and nurse their young, have hinged backbones, hair, and a four-chambered heart, *and* maintain a constant internal body temperature. (This means mammals are *homoiothermic*. Reptiles and amphibians, in contrast, depend on their outside environment for body heat.) Most mammals give birth to live young, but a few—echidnas and platypuses, for instance—are egg-laying.

Out of roughly 1 million known animal species on the planet, about 4,300 species are mammals. This may sound like a lot, but compare it with 20,000 species of fishes or 100,000 species of insects. So mammals belong to a very small (but important) club. Without other mammals, humans would probably not survive, and we'd certainly be overwhelmed by legions of insects.

To keep track of the millions of animal and plant species on Earth, scientists use a universal system called taxonomy. Taxonomy starts with the five main groups of all living things, the kingdoms, and then divides those into the next group down—phylum, then class, order, family, genus, and, finally, species. Members of a species look similar and can reproduce with each other.

For an example of how taxonomy works, follow the highlighted lines above to see how the pipistrelle bat, *Pipistrellus pipistrellus*, is classified. In this book, the scientific name of each animal is listed next to the common name. The first word is the genus. The second word is the species.

Turn to the glossarized index at the back of this book if you're looking for a specific animal, or for special information (what's a proboscis, for instance), or for the definition of a word you don't understand.

TASMANIAN DEVIL *(Sarcophilus harrisii)*

MARY SUNDSTROM

Sporting blackish-brown fur, white patches on its rump, and a pink snout, ears, feet, and tail, the Tasmanian devil might be mistaken for a tiny bear. This pouched mammal moves slowly, even clumsily. It is a predator— not a very skilled one, though— and a nifty scavenger. The Tasmanian devil feeds mainly on rabbits, wombats, wallabies, and sheep, mostly as carrion (the flesh of dead animals). (It also eats poisonous snakes!) It is equipped with a strong jaw and bone-crushing teeth, the better to eat fur and bones. To find its food, the Tasmanian devil depends on a keen sense of smell and may sniff the ground like a dog. Although this critter prefers solid ground, it is able to climb trees.

Tasmanian devils are active at night. By day they prefer to hide out in grassy, leafy burrows or inside hollow logs and caves. They also seem to enjoy sunbathing.

The Tasmanian devil lives only in Tasmania. Long ago, its range probably included much of Australia, but that was before the dingo, a wild dog, was introduced Down Under and competed with the Tasmanian devil for food.

Although the Tasmanian devil has a reputation for a devilish temper, some scientists say those tantrums are exaggerated. Nevertheless, Tasmanian devils are definitely aggressive with each other.

The Tasmanian devil once scavenged the remains of animals killed by the great Tasmanian wolf, a carnivore that is now extinct.

Photo, facing page courtesy Animals Animals © M. Austerman

BETH EVANS

MAMMALS

STAR-NOSED MOLE (Condylura cristata)

Is it a starfish on four legs? A space monster? A mutant ninja rodent? Well, actually, it's a star-nosed mole. This critter boasts 22 extremely weird fleshy rays (tentacles) that sprout from its muzzle. Its eyes are small, its ears barely show, and its tail is scaly and sparsely haired. Each spring, the star-nosed mole's tail increases to the size of a #2 pencil; the extra fat provides energy during the mating season.

Star-nosed moles are expert swimmers and divers. They use all four feet to paddle, and they can even cruise under ice in winter. Their dense blackish-brown fur acts like a wet suit and is partly water repellent. Star-nosed moles collect food—aquatic insects, crustaceans, and small fishes—on the bottom of ponds and streams. To grab a bite, all but the star-nosed mole's top two nose tentacles are constantly in motion.

Of course, star-nosed moles can eat on land, too. A favorite meal is lots of juicy earthworms. For this reason, some gardeners and farmers consider them pests.

Star-nosed moles live in small colonies, and within each family group, the male and female winter together. In the spring, the female gives birth to a litter of from two to seven young. These youngsters seem independent at the age of three weeks. Could you imagine having to earn a living at that age?

Star-nosed moles live in North America all the way from Manitoba, Canada, south to Georgia. They measure about 15 to 20 centimeters (6 to 8 inches) from head to tip of tail.

Did anyone ever tell you, "Don't make a mountain out of a molehill?" Star-nosed moles live in burrows underground. They prefer muddy soil, and when they unearth tunnels, molehills are formed. Star-nosed moles usually stay underground during the day and come out at night.

Photo, facing page: courtesy Animals animals. © Michael Habicht

MAMMALS

PROBOSCIS MONKEY (Nasalis larvatus)

If the nose knows, then a male proboscis monkey knows all because his nose just doesn't stop growing. In fact, it may reach a length of 10 centimeters (about 4 inches)—so long, it overhangs his mouth. To female monkeys, the longer the male's nose, the stronger the sex appeal.

With such a long schnozz, is it any wonder the proboscis monkey kee-honks when it is happily devouring shoots, leaves, and assorted fruits? To snooze, adults stretch out on their backs while their young swing from grown-ups' tails or squeeze the biggest nose that's handy.

Proboscis monkeys love to get into the swim. They high-dive 15 meters (about 50 feet) from trees, swim under water, and then dogpaddle across streams, lakes, and even in oceans. Waterlogged proboscis monkeys have been rescued far from ocean shores by fishing boats.

Proboscis monkeys may grow to a height of 76 centimeters ($2^1/_2$ feet not counting their tail), and they may weigh as much as 22 kilograms (about 50 pounds). They live in very flexible social groups.

Although the button-eyed male proboscis monkeys are famous for their heroic noses and pinkish-brown faces, their young are born with deep blue faces and tiny noses.

Proboscis monkeys get their name from a Latin word for an elephant's trunk. Their noses are fleshy and flexible, and some are so long they get in the way when these animals drink or eat.

The nose of the male proboscis monkey keeps growing, and growing, and growing its whole life. Because females prefer to mate with the longest-nosed males, evolution ensures that proboscis monkeys will remain the Cyranos of the rain forest.

MAMMALS

WARTHOG (*Phacochoerus aethiopicus*)

Even with a mouthful of tusks and a hide covered with bristles and warts, there's something debonair about the warthog. Although it is generally mild-mannered, a warthog will defend itself when necessary. Its tusks can cause severe injuries. The big upper tusks look dangerous, but the lower—smaller and sharper—pair do the most damage.

Warthogs live in Africa south of the Sahara Desert, especially where the land is grassy or lightly forested. When grazing, they often shuffle along on their padded wrists. They are usually active during the day, except in areas where they are hunted by humans. Then they come out only after dark.

To raise their young (piglets), and sleep, and hide out, warthogs use natural holes or aardvark burrows. They often live in "clans" of four to 16 members, although adult males usually keep to themselves.

During the mating season, male warthogs do battle with other males. They butt tusks and heads together, and the warts on each side of their head cushion the blows.

When a warthog is relaxed, or munching on grass, roots, berries, or bark, its tail hangs down. On the run, a warthog's tail rises straight up like a wiry flagpole.

MAMMALS

DOUROUCOULI *(Aotus trivirgatus)*

Put on your thinking cap. What do bush babies, sakis, monkeys, apes, chimpanzees, and *you* all have in common? The answer is right in the palm of your primate hands and fingers. Each animal on the list is a member of the scientific order Primates, and all primates have flexible hands with grasping digits, or fingers (usually ten of them). They also have a relatively large brain and a tree-dwelling lifestyle at some point in their evolution.

Douroucoulis are monkeys—they're sometimes called night monkeys—and they live deep in the tropical forests of Venezuela and Brazil. By day, douroucoulis may hang out in leafy nests tucked in tree hollows or ropy vines. By night, they burst into acrobatic action, speeding over tree branches, leaping, and swinging.

These monkeys dine on fruits, nuts, leaves, flowers, bark, insects, and assorted small vertebrates (animals who have backbones) such as lizards and frogs.

Family groups consist of two to five members, including the adult pair, who usually have one young each year. Unfortunately, like many primate species, douroucoulis are in danger of becoming extinct. They are hunted for their fur, which is semi-woolly and extremely soft. They are also collected for the "pet" trade and biomedical research. But the biggest threat to these monkeys is loss of living space, or habitat.

Douroucoulis are vocal critters known to communicate using fifty or so different sounds including squeaks, hisses, and barks. When alarmed, they inflate their throat sacs to create a deep "wook, wook, wook!"

Photo, facing page, courtesy Animals Animals © Michael Dick

M A M M A L S

THREE-TOED SLOTH *(Bradypus tridactylus)*

Hanging out is nothing unusual for the three-toed sloth. In fact, this critter spends most of its life in trees hanging from limbs or sitting in branch forks in the forests of southern Venezuela, the Guianas, and northern Brazil.

The three-toed sloth stays in one tree—especially the cecropia—for long periods. It carefully picks tender leaves, twigs, and buds to eat.

These sloths do come down to the ground but only once or twice a week. When they are grounded, they urinate and defecate and then move to the next tree. Because their terrestrial form of locomotion is a slow crawl, they risk attack by predators. They use their sharp claws to defend themselves and also to climb and to grasp food.

Most of the time, three-toed sloths move extremely sloooowly. For this reason, they depend on a swivel neck so they can be on the lookout for enemies. One or two extra neck vertebrae (bones) gives them 270-degree turning power—about three-quarters of a circle. Compare that to your own ability to twist your neck 180 degrees or so—half a circle.

Because many of the trees are being cut down where three-toed sloths live, they are endangered by loss of habitat.

Young three-toed sloths are carried on their mother's abdomen for months until they feed on their own.

The three-toed sloth has grayish-brown fur and brown speckles on its shoulders. If this sloth appears to be green, that's because algae sometimes grows on its coat.

Photo facing page courtesy Animals Animals © Raymond A Mendez

MAMMALS

SILKY ANTEATER *(Cyclopes didactylus)*

The silky anteater may devour between 700 and 5,000 ants (count 'em) per night depending on its size, age, and sex. Its long, tacky, wormlike tongue is made to stick to ants, termites, and some other insects.

Silky anteaters live in tropical forests from southern Mexico to Bolivia and Brazil. By day, they rest in shady spots under leaves and vines; by night, they go to work. Treetops are great places to find insects and termites, and silk-cotton treetops are best of all. That's because these trees have seed pods that are soft and silvery and provide excellent camouflage.

While silky anteaters prey on creepy crawlies, harpy eagles and owls prey on silky anteaters. To defend themselves, silky anteaters raise up on their hind legs, grasp tree branches with their feet, wrap their prehensile (grasping) tails around twigs, and extend the claws on their forefeet. Unfortunately, this threat posture doesn't always offer much protection.

Silky anteaters are named for their soft, silky golden hair. They sport pink noses, black eyes, reddish feet, and sharp, curved claws on their second and third fingers.

Silky anteaters make a tree-hole nest of dry leaves for their young. The single off-spring is raised by both parents, who feed it partially digested insects.

The National Wildlife Federation is the nation's largest conservation organization. For more than fifty years, NWF has worked to conserve wildlife and its habitat. NWF was instrumental in obtaining enactment of the Endangered Species Act in 1973 and has continued working to defend and strengthen that important environmental law. Write: NWF, 1400 16th Street, N.W., Washington, D.C. 20036.

MAMMALS

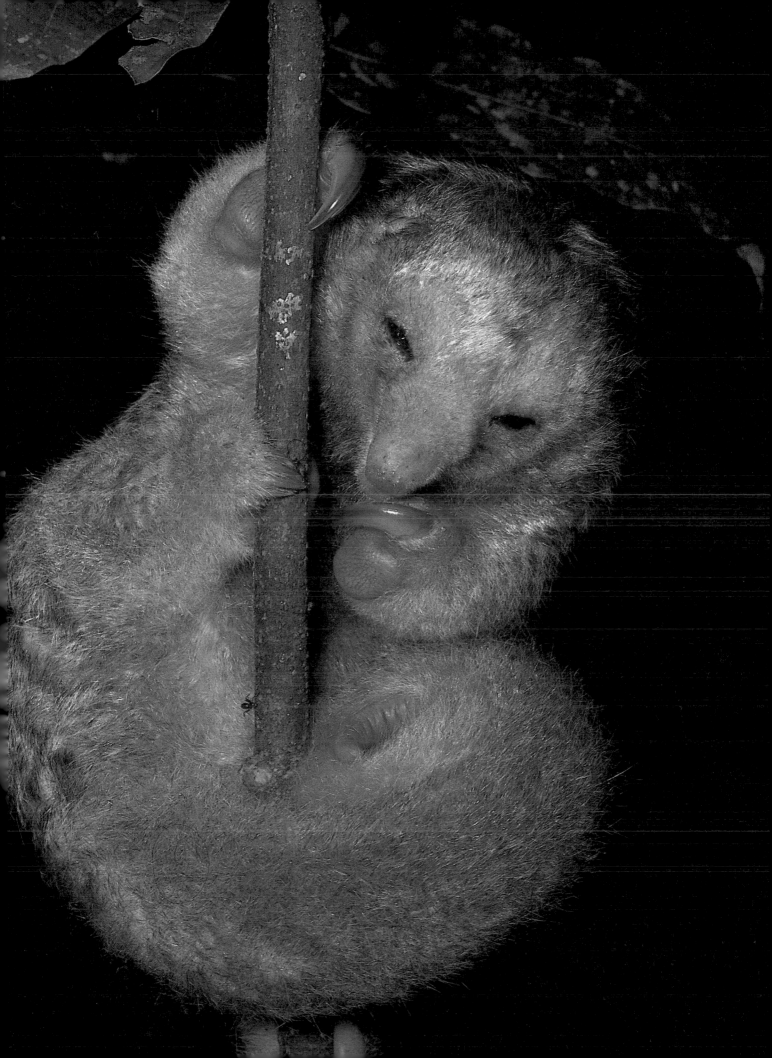

PIPISTRELLE BAT *(Pipistrellus pipistrellus)*

Lots of mammals can jump, trot, skip, and swim, but bats are the only mammals that can fly. In fact, some can reach an airspeed of more than 96 kilometers (60 miles) per hour and an altitude of more than 3 kilometers (10,000 feet). Not every kind of bat can do that. Since there are more than 900 bat species worldwide, it's not surprising that each has its own specialized abilities. Some bats devour insects by the pound, others dine solely on fruit, and still others prefer frogs, birds, and even blood!

Bats vary in size from the largest, the flying fox, which has a wingspan of more than 152 centimeters (5 feet), to the most minuscule, the bumblebee bat, which is only 12 centimeters (5 inches) across with wings outstretched and weighs less than a dime.

Bats are extremely important in the balance of nature. Because they pollinate, reseed, and help control insect populations, you might call them nature's gardeners.

The pipistrelle bat lives in Europe, Algeria, Libya, and Morocco. It is an insectivorous bat, which is a long way of saying it dines on insects. Like most bats, the pipistrelle flies out of its roost at dusk and hunts almost all night long. By day, it roosts in trees, caves, or even under the eaves of buildings.

Dracula, vampire, ghost, demon! Because bats hunt at night in complete darkness, superstitious people have long feared their "supernatural" powers. As we learn more about the world, bats have revealed their non-aggressive nature, and their "supernatural" powers have turned out to be extremely natural!

Bat Conservation International (BCI) can give you more information on bats. This nonprofit organization funds worldwide bat education and conservation projects. They also publish *BATS*, a newsletter for members of all ages. For a donation of any size, you can receive easy-to-follow bat house plans. Write to BCI at P.O. Box 162603, Austin, TX 78716.

Photo, facing page, courtesy Animals Animals © Richard Packwood

MAMMALS

GENET *(Genetta genetta)*

Deep in a rocky burrow in the forests and on the grasslands and plains of Europe and Africa, the genet sleeps away its day. At night, in contrast, this small meat-eater (carnivore) might climb trees to hunt for nesting and roosting birds, although most of its prey is captured on the ground. The genet seems to glide over the earth. That's because it walks on its digits in what has been described as a "waltzing trot."

Genets usually travel alone or in pairs. They communicate with each other using a variety of vocal and visual signals. They also have a keen sense of smell. Like skunks, genets can send smelly messages from the anal scent glands located on their rear ends.

You might think of the genet as a distant relative of the mongoose, although some scientists believe the mongoose belongs to its very own family. Both have short legs, a pointy snout, and a long tail, but the genet looks more like a cat than the mongoose does.

If a genet can fit its head through an opening, its body can always follow. That's because its body is slender and loosely jointed.

Genets have retractable claws—they extend and recede—the better to catch frogs, lizards, rodents, insects, spiders, and even fruit, bulbs, and nuts. Some genets eat carrion.

MAMMALS

MUSK-OX *(Ovibus moschatus)*

To look at the thick, matted fur of the musk-ox, you might think it's a very old critter. Indeed, this single living species has been around for a very long time. Two-thousand-year-old fossil remains of the musk-ox are regularly found in northwestern Siberia.

Both the male and female musk-ox sport broad, curving horns. The base of the horns almost meets in the middle—something like a Viking helmet.

The musk-ox lives only in Arctic tundra, and it depends on the thick, coarse hairs that cover it from head to hoof to shed rain and snow. A dense inner layer of soft hair serves as insulation to keep frost out.

Musk-ox are sociable animals, and they usually travel in herds of 10 to 20 members (although they may number as many as 100!) in search of food. During long winter months, they eat crowberry, cowberry, and willow. When the weather warms up, they browse on grass and sedges.

Although musk-ox look big and tough, they must defend themselves against predators. To do this, they form a circle (heads usually facing outward) around their young. This is a good form of protection from predators such as wolves but not against humans; entire herds have been destroyed by human hunters.

The musk-ox is named for the musky odor given off by males during the rut, or mating season.

Each summer, adult bulls (males) battle to determine who will be leader of the herd. Their fights last for more than 45 minutes and may include head-on collisions at 40 kilometers (25 miles) per hour. During their battles, they bellow and roar.

MAMMALS

SOUTHERN ELEPHANT SEAL (*Mirounga leonina*)

What weighs 3,700 kilograms (8,157 pounds), is 600 centimeters (19 feet) long, and has a trunklike, inflatable proboscis that hangs over its mouth? A male elephant seal, of course. During the breeding season, the male elephant seal's proboscis swells up (from air and increased blood pressure) until it looks like a large cushion. Inflation aims the seal's nostrils into its mouth so its snorts echo. This inflatable organ may also serve as an amplifier to enhance the bull's roar.

It may take anywhere from three days to an entire month for elephant seals to molt or shed their fur coat. During this time, they don't eat anything.

Southern elephant seals breed on the sandy beaches of most subantarctic islands and on the coast of southern Argentina. All seals spend long periods at sea when they're not resting, molting (shedding fur), or breeding on land.

The southern elephant seal has very flexible flippers—the better for scooping sand and swimming. It can make holes in the ice with its head and swim 20 kilometers (12 miles) under ice, where it breathes only in air pockets. It's also a nifty diver, able to spend more than 30 minutes underwater! The elephant seal swims at a top speed of 25 kilometers per hour (15 mph) and dines on fishes and cephalopods, including octopuses, squid, and cuttlefishes.

According to fossil records, elephant seals have probably weighed as much as 5,000 kilograms (11,023 pounds) and reached a length of 900 centimeters (29 feet)!

MAMMALS

SPOTTED HYENA *(Crocuta crocuta)*

Spotted hyenas boast jaws that may be the most powerful for their size of any living mammal. That's all the better for devouring entire carcasses—skin *and* bones—of wildebeests, zebras, and other prey. In fact, each spotted hyena can devour 14.5 kilograms (about 31 pounds!) of food per meal.

Although they are able hunters (often running in packs of 10 to 25 members), spotted hyenas also scavenge for carrion, which makes them part of nature's recycling project.

A spotted hyena sports black-brown spots on its coarse, yellowish fur. The female is larger than the male, and that's important because she is also the leader of the pack.

Spotted hyenas live on the open plains and rocky lowlands of Africa south of the Sahara Desert. They spend their days in deserted aardvark holes or natural cave dens. At twilight they emerge to begin the night's work. On the hunt, spotted hyenas average 40 to 50 kilometers per hour (about 30 mph), although their maximum speed is 60 kilometers per hour (37 mph).

Some humans consider the hyena beneficial because it is a scavenger. For other humans, the hyena is viewed with superstitious fear. Some tribes put their dead out for hyenas to eat.

The "laughing" hyena gives its famous spine-tingling laugh when it's being chased or attacked.

SNUB-NOSED MONKEY (*Rhinopithecus roxellana*)

Monkeys are primates that can be divided into two large groups: Old World and New World. New World monkeys live in South and Central America. Some have prehensile tails that can reach and grab like a third arm. None have tough "sitting pads" on their rear ends like Old World monkeys.

Old World monkeys live in Africa, Southeast Asia, and the Malay Archipelago. They have tough pads (like calluses) on their rumps so they can sleep sitting up in trees.

Snub-nosed monkeys, who live in the high mountain forests of China, belong to the Old World group. They spend most of their time in trees—and head straight for the high branches when frightened—but they do come down to the ground to feed and socialize.

Tender fir and pine needles as well as bamboo shoots, fruits, buds, and leaves are all part of the snub-nosed monkey's diet. Food isn't always easy to find, because this monkey lives in snowy weather at least half the year.

Although snub-nosed monkeys are known to travel in troops of 100 to 600 individuals, there are probably smaller groups of four to six adults and their young within each troop.

When snub-nosed monkeys happen on a good source of food, they say it loud: "Ga-ga!"

Captive primates can be more aggressive than their relatives in the wild. That's because they are forced to live in small spaces and compete for food. Human primates in big cities are usually more aggressive and grumpy than their country cousins.

In the Middle Ages, physicians dissected the bodies of monkeys so they could learn more about human anatomy. In those days, dissecting a human body for medical purposes was strictly against the rules.

MAMMALS

BAIRD'S TAPIR *(Tapirus bairdii)*

Ungulates are mammals that have hooves. Odd-toed ungulates come in a variety of sizes, shapes, and colors. What they have in common is the hard, bony hoof at the end of their legs and their toe count—an odd number. Rhinoceroses, horses, and tapirs are all odd-toed mammals. They look very different, but they are related.

Baird's tapir sports a brown coat that fits right in—with its surroundings, that is. This animal is dark reddish-brown on top and usually lighter below. Its shady coloring provides camouflage in the forests of southern Mexico, Colombia, and Ecuador.

Tapirs live in the lowlands where they are able to find lots of water. They like to wallow in shallow rivers, and that may help them shake off mites, ticks, and other parasites.

Fossil remains prove that tapirs haven't changed much for many millions of years. All four species still have a short trunk of a nose (and a keen sense of smell). They have four toes on their front feet and three toes on the back. Tapirs can grow to a weight of 226 kilograms (500 pounds) and a length of 250 centimeters (about 8 feet).

Shy, docile tapirs are nocturnal critters: they sleep the day away and do their "work" at night.

Tapirs are nifty runners, waders, sliders, divers, and swimmers. Their shape allows them to move quickly through underbrush.

MAMMALS

GREATER KUDU *(Tragelaphus strepsiceros)*

Even-toed ungulates (hoofed mammals)—warthogs, camels, deer, and kudus, for instance—all have a hard, bony hoof at the end of their legs and an even toe count. Male kudus (and their relatives, bushbucks, bongos, and nyalas) also sport amazing twisted horns.

Young greater kudus are called "calves."

Take a closer look at the greater kudu's horns: they often measure about 132 centimeters (52 inches) along the curves. During the rut, or mating season, the male greater kudu may link horns with another male to compete for a female partner. The opponents push and twist and try to shove each other off balance. Two horns provide some protection for the greater kudu, but they also offer a big disadvantage: they are prized by human trophy hunters.

Greater kudus live in areas of Africa from southern Chad to Somalia to South Africa. They prefer woodlands where they browse on leaves and grass and take cover day or night. They depend on their keen hearing to avoid predators, and they are exceptional athletes, able to leap over bushes that are 2.5 meters (8 feet) high. Greater kudus do have a dangerous habit of stopping to look over their shoulder. This can prove fatal if a predator is in pursuit.

Male bushbucks—close relatives of greater kudus—use their horns to fight each other during the rut (mating season). They charge, lock horns, and even stab opponents.

MAMMALS

NAKED MOLE-RAT (*Heterocephalus glaber*)

The mole-rat's wrinkled pinkish-yellowish skin looks naked at first glance. Look again: a few pale hairs sprout from its chunky head, body and tail, its lips are whiskered, and its feet are fringed. The hairs on the naked mole-rat's feet act as tiny brooms that collect and sweep away loose dirt during digging.

Naked mole rats are adapted to the dirty life. Colonies of twenty to thirty members build nifty burrow systems underground. One system can stretch for 300 meters (almost 1,000 feet!) and includes a community nest chamber as well as many entrances and exits and rooms for emergencies.

To dig their tunnels, mole-rats form a relay line. The rat at the earth's surface loosens the soil and kicks it backward to the next rat in line, who kicks it to the next, and so on. When enough dirt is collected deep in the tunnel, the inside rat backs its way to the surface. As it moves out—and the others move up—it pushes earth with its hind feet. One by one, the mole-rats push out the earth. If you happened upon a naked mole-rat burrow construction site, you'd see dirt flying in all directions.

Naked mole-rats are found in Ethiopia, Somalia, and Kenya.

A female naked mole-rat always leads the colony while younger naked mole-rats act as workers.

Of all mammals, naked mole-rats have the hardest time maintaining a constant internal body temperature. To avoid exhaustion, they only construct or remodel their burrows during the early mornings and late afternoons when the temperature is moderate.

Photo: feeding pose, courtesy Animals Animals © Raymond A. Mendez

MAMMALS

HAIRY ARMADILLO *(Chaetophractus villosus)*

Armored in a double layer of horn and bone, the hairy armadillo looks as weird as other armadillos—only hairier. How does the hairy armadillo develop its armor? A baby armadillo is born with tough, leathery skin that hardens into horny plates or bands as it grows. This armored shell is very handy for hiding from other animals. And because the plates are surrounded by flexible skin, armadillos of some species can roll up into a ball when threatened. That's good protection for an armadillo's belly, which is covered with soft skin and hair instead of scales.

Adult hairy armadillos may measure as much as 57 centimeters (about 2 feet) from head to tail's end and weigh as much as 2 kilograms (4½ pounds). They live in open areas of northern Paraguay and parts of Bolivia and Argentina.

Hairy armadillos burrow under dead animals to munch on maggots and other insects. They also kill small snakes by hurling themselves on the reptile's body and cutting it with the edges of their armor.

The tongue of the giant armadillo—a relative of the hairy armadillo—is shaped like a worm, and it has many small bumps covered with sticky saliva. These sticky bumps are great for catching ants, worms, spiders, and insects. But the giant armadillo's favorite food treat is a mouthful of termites. Because giant armadillos have claws and powerful limbs, they are very good diggers and scratchers. They can tear up termite hills in search of food and leave holes so big a human can fit inside.

Photo, facing page: courtesy Animals Animals © Michael Dick

MAMMALS

Jumping Kangaroo

RED KANGAROO (*Macropus rufus*)

Kangaroos, wallabies, opossums, and bandicoots are members of the scientific order *Marsupialia*; they're commonly called marsupials. Marsupials are different from all other mammals because they have special features of reproduction. Most female marsupials have an abdominal (belly) pouch in which they carry their young. Some species of marsupials develop a pouch only during reproduction, and some pouches are just an extra fold of skin. After marsupial young are born, they crawl into their mother's pouch where they nurse—for weeks or even months!—before emerging.

Giant red kangaroos are the biggest marsupials in the world. They may measure 280 centimeters (about 9 feet) from their head to the tip of their tail and weigh almost 90 kilograms (200 pounds). They live on the grass-covered plains of Australia, and like all kangaroos, they are herbivores (plant-eaters).

Red kangaroos live in organized groups called "mobs." A mob usually consists of two to ten individuals, but many mobs may gather at the same water hole during dry seasons.

The red kangaroo depends on its strong hindquarters to keep it leaping and hopping. Its tail acts as a rudder for balance during leaps, and it makes a third leg for sitting. The tail is so strong, it can support the red kangaroo's entire weight. Indeed, when they move slowly, kangaroos use a "five-footed" gait: they balance on their forearms and tail as they swing their hind legs forward. At high speed, kangaroos can leap 9 meters (29 feet) or more.

Within one day after a young red kangaroo leaves its mother's pouch, another baby may be born.

The red kangaroo is the world's largest marsupial; still, a red kangaroo newborn weighs less than one gram (.035 ounce) at birth.

All species of kangaroos are most active at twilight or at night. They often feed from late afternoon to early morning and rest during daylight hours.

Photo, facing page, courtesy Animals Animals © Michael Dick

MAMMALS

COYPU *(Myocastor coypus)*

The coypu (a.k.a. the nutria) looks a lot like a large brown rat: its eyes and ears are small, its claws are sharp, and its incisor teeth are bright orange. Bright orange? That's no rat.

This semiaquatic rodent lives in marshes and on the banks of lakes and streams in southern Brazil, Bolivia, Paraguay, Uruguay, Argentina, and Chile. Although the coypu, a strict vegetarian, can get around on land, it's most at home in the water, where it browses on water plants. It has webbed hind feet to aid water locomotion.

Coypus usually breed year-round, and females produce two or three litters of one to 13 young. Newborn coypus weigh about 200 grams (about 7 ounces) and are furry and wide-eyed. Fully grown coypus may weigh in at 10 kilograms (22 pounds).

Coypus love life in the water, and they often make grassy platforms or rafts where they hang out, eat, and groom themselves.

Not only does the coypu have bright orange front teeth but those teeth never stop growing! *All* **rodents have four front teeth that grow for a lifetime. These teeth are worn down by daily use. There's also a gap between tooth rows so that the rodent can gnaw with its mouth closed!**

MAMMALS

AFRICAN PORCUPINE *(Hystrix africaeaustralis)*

This Old World porcupine is covered with blackish quills—very sharp, stiff hairs—banded with white. It also sports a shortish tail tipped with rattle quills that produce lots of noise. When alarmed, this prickly rodent will fan and rattle its spines, stamp its feet, and charge backward in an effort to "stick" its enemy. It has been known to injure and even kill lions, hyenas, and humans.

The prickly porcupine's quills may grow to a length of 35 centimeters (more than 13 inches). That's a lot of sticking power.

Old World porcupines run with a shuffling, clumsy gait when they're frightened.

African porcupines prefer life in deserts, grasslands, and forests in the southern half of Africa. They take shelter in caves, crevices, and borrowed burrows; they also make their own dugout homes, which they line with grass.

Nighttime is the right time to find African porcupines searching for roots, bulbs, and tubers to eat. They may also feed on insects and carrion and gnaw on bones. Although they rarely climb trees, African porcupines are nifty swimmers.

The female African porcupine gives birth to a litter of one to four young, born with open eyes and short, soft quills.

MAMMALS

AARDVARK (*Orycteropus afer*)

The aardvark looks a bit like a humpbacked pig. It has extremely thick skin and bristly gray hairs. Its piglike snout is whiskered, and its waxy ears can move in separate directions at the same time. The aardvark depends on its long, sticky tongue to gather termites and ants to eat. (When the aardvark's tongue is not in use, it curls up at the end like a coil spring.)

A keen sense of smell helps aarvarks sniff out termite nests and anthills, which they dig up. They also have sharp ears—the better to listen for insects on the move. A column of marching termites may stretch a distance of about 40 meters (130 feet!), and that many termites make a lot of noise.

Because it burrows, the aardvark is considered a pest—and is killed—by many farmers. But farmers have learned that when there are no aardvarks to control the termite population, termites may devour farm crops.

Aardvarks live in much of Africa. "Aardvark" is Afrikaans for "earth pig," and indeed this piglike critter is an energetic burrower.

In soft earth, aardvarks can dig quicker than several kids with shovels!

MAMMALS

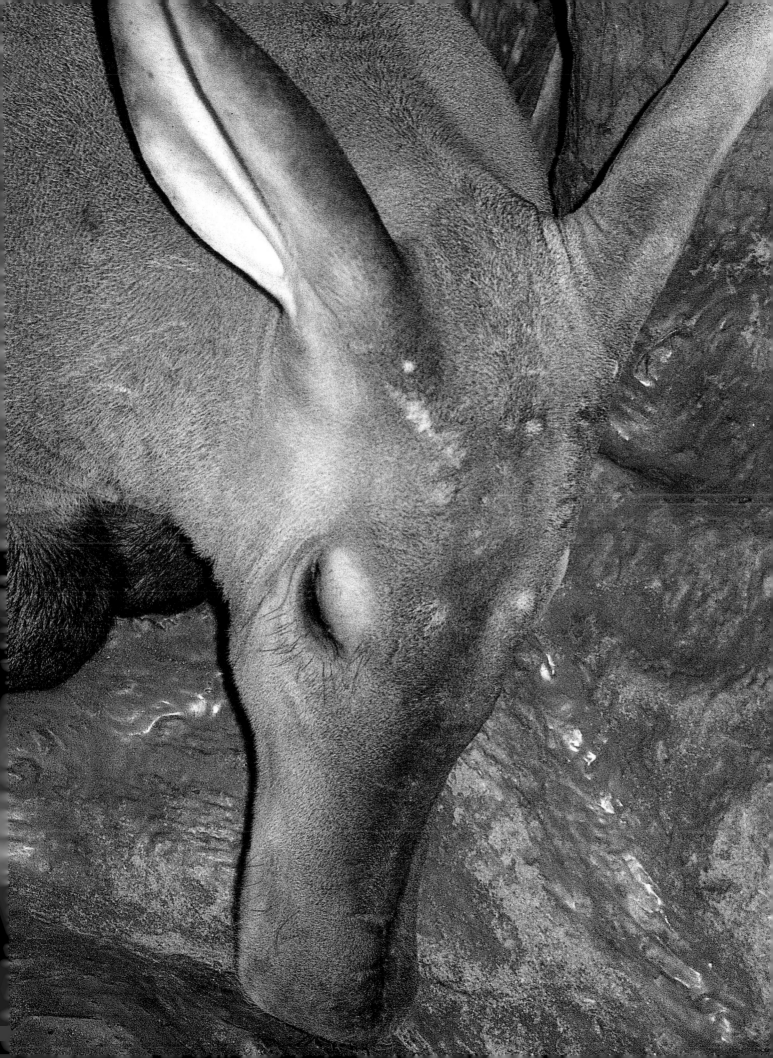

DUCK-BILLED PLATYPUS (*Ornithorhynchus anatinus*)

What has a duck's bill and duck's feet, a bear's claws, and a beaver's tail? The duck-billed platypus, of course. This extremely weird-looking mammal lives in the freshwater streams, lakes, and lagoons of Australia and Tasmania.

The platypus is a nifty digger, diver, and swimmer. It spends much of its time in water where it feeds mainly on crayfish, snails, shrimp, worms, tadpoles, insect larvae, and small fish.

When the platypus swims underwater, it can't see or hear because its ears and eyes are covered by skin folds. To navigate and find food, it depends on its sense of touch and its very sensitive bill, which may be able to sense muscle activity in prey.

Platypuses build two kinds of burrows in stream banks and along shorelines. One is used by both males and females. The other is made by the female to rear her young. Two weeks after mating, she lays one to three eggs in a nest made of damp leaves. After about ten days, the young hatch blind and naked. Within four months, they emerge from the burrow fully furred. Newly hatched platypuses are about 25 millimeters (less than 1 inch) long. Adults reach a head-to-tail length of about 45 centimeters (17 inches).

A platypus hatches with its own wet suit and fins—almost. Its coarse top fur and its thick woolly under fur (which traps air) provide insulation and warmth just like a wet suit. Its webbed feet give it paddling power in water. On land, the webbed area on each forefoot folds back under five claws.

On their hind legs, male platypuses have hollow spurs which, when raised, can inject venom into other animals. The venom is used mainly against other male platypuses when competing for mates or for territory. The effects of the venom are strong enough to kill a dog and to cause extreme pain in humans.

MAMMALS

This glossarized index will help you find specific information about mammals. It will also help you understand the meaning of some of the words used in this book.

XTREMELY WEIRD SERIES

All of the titles are written by Sarah Lovett, 8½" x 11", 48 pages, $9.95 paperback, $14.95 hardcover, with or photographs and illustrations.

remely Weird Bats
remely Weird Birds
remely Weird Endangered Species
remely Weird Fishes
remely Weird Frogs
remely Weird Insects
remely Weird Mammals
remely Weird Micro Monsters
remely Weird Primates
remely Weird Reptiles
remely Weird Sea Creatures
remely Weird Snakes
remely Weird Spiders

RAY VISION SERIES

ach title in the series is 8½" x 11", 48 pages, $9.95 paperback, with color photographs and illustrations, d written by Ron Schultz.

king Inside the Brain
king Inside Cartoon Animation
king Inside Caves and Caverns
king Inside Sports Aerodynamics
king Inside Sunken Treasure
king Inside Telescopes and the Night Sky

THE KIDDING AROUND TRAVEL GUIDES

All of the titles listed below are 64 pages and $9.95 paperbacks, except for *Kidding Around the National Parks* and *Kidding Around Spain*, which are 108 pages and $12.95 paperbacks.

Kidding Around Atlanta
Kidding Around Boston, 2nd ed.
Kidding Around Chicago, 2nd ed.
Kidding Around the Hawaiian Islands
Kidding Around London
Kidding Around Los Angeles
Kidding Around the National Parks
of the Southwest
Kidding Around New York City, 2nd ed.
Kidding Around Paris
Kidding Around Philadelphia
Kidding Around San Diego
Kidding Around San Francisco
Kidding Around Santa Fe
Kidding Around Seattle
Kidding Around Spain
Kidding Around Washington, D.C., 2nd ed.

MASTERS OF MOTION SERIES

Each title in the series is 10¼" x 9", 48 pages, $9.95 paperback, with color photographs and illustrations.

How to Drive an Indy Race Car
David Rubel
How to Fly a 747
Tim Paulson
How to Fly the Space Shuttle
Russell Shorto

THE KIDS EXPLORE SERIES

Each title is written by kids for kids by the Westridge Young Writers Workshop, 7" x 9", and $9.95 paperback, with photographs and illustrations by the kids.

Kids Explore America's Hispanic Heritage
112 pages
Kids Explore America's African American Heritage 128 pages
Kids Explore the Gifts of Children with Special Needs 128 pages
Kids Explore America's Japanese American Heritage 144 pages

ENVIRONMENTAL TITLES

Habitats: *Where the Wild Things Live*
Randi Hacker and Jackie Kaufman
8½" x 11", 48 pages, color illustrations, $9.95 paper

The Indian Way: *Learning to Communicate with Mother Earth*
Gary McLain
7" x 9", 114 pages, two-color illustrations, $9.95 paper

Rads, Ergs, and Cheeseburgers: *The Kids' Guide to Energy and the Environment*
Bill Yanda
7" x 9", 108 pages, two-color illustrations, $13.95 paper

The Kids' Environment Book: *What's Awry and Why*
Anne Pedersen
7" x 9", 192 pages, two-color illustrations, $13.95 paper

BIZARRE & BEAUTIFUL SERIES

A spirited and fun investigation of the mysteries of the five senses in the animal kingdom.

Each title in the series is 8½" x 11", $9.95 paperback, $14.95 hardcover, with color photographs and illustrations throughout.

Bizarre & Beautiful Ears
Bizarre & Beautiful Eyes
Bizarre & Beautiful Feelers
Bizarre & Beautiful Noses
Bizarre & Beautiful Tongues

RAINBOW WARRIOR SERIES

W hat is a Rainbow Warrior Artist? It is a person who strives to live in harmony with the Earth and all living creatures, and who tries to better the world while living his or her life in a creative way.

Each title is written by Reavis Moore with a foreword by LeVar Burton, and is 8½" x 11", 48 pages, $14.95 hardcover, with color photographs and illustrations.

Native Artists of Africa
Native Artists of North America
Native Artists of Europe

ROUGH AND READY SERIES

L earn about the men and women who settled the American West. Explore the myths and legends about these courageous individuals and learn about the environmental, cultural, and economic legacies they left to us.

Each title in the series is written by A. S. Gintzler and is 48 pages, 8½" x 11", $12.95 hardcover, with two-color illustrations and duotone archival photographs.

Rough and Ready Cowboys
Rough and Ready Homesteaders
Rough and Ready Loggers

Rough and Ready
 Outlaws & Lawmen
Rough and Ready Prospectors
Rough and Ready Railroaders

AMERICAN ORIGINS SERIES

M any of us are the third and fourth generation of our families to live in America. Learn what our great-grandparents experienced when they arrived here and how much of our lives are still intertwined with theirs.

Each title is 48 pages, 8½" x 11", $12.95 hardcover, with two-color illustrations and duotone archival photographs.

Tracing Our English Roots
Tracing Our French Roots
Tracing Our German Roots
Tracing Our Irish Roots

Tracing Our Italian Roots
Tracing Our Japanese Roots
Tracing Our Jewish Roots
Tracing Our Polish Roots